# Landscapes Old and New

## ALSO BY ALLEN IRELAND

*Loners and Mothers*
*Dark and Light Verse*

# Landscapes Old and New

*Poems by Allen Lee Ireland*

David Robert Books

Published by David Robert Books
P.O. Box 541106
Cincinnati, OH 45254-1106

ISBN: 9781625494658

Poetry Editor: Kevin Walzer
Business Editor: Lori Jareo

Visit us on the web at www.davidrobertbooks.com

Photos for this book were taken from Battle Branch Road in Bryson City, North Carolina, by the author.

# Acknowledgments

Speaking as a relatively unknown poet, rejected ten times more than he's been accepted, I am always grateful to any print or online publication that gives a poem of mine a place to shine, such as the ones listed below. There are old and new poems in this book, thus the title. The old poems, some of them slightly altered, are from my two previous collections.

*Beyond Queer Words:* "Roadside Example"

*The Lyric:* "World of Water"

*The Orchards Poetry Journal:* "Two Trees"

*The Rising Phoenix Review:* "Creek Rock," "Red-tailed Hawk"

*The Road Not Taken:* "Anastasia's Boy"

*Smoky Mountain Times:* "Octogenarian"

*Sparks of Calliope:* "Lighthouse Murder," "Tableau"

*WestWard Quarterly:* "Truck Care"

# Table of Contents

*This book is dedicated to all the landscapes of my childhood,
in appreciation of the companionship they gave me.*

It's resting-time, I'm old.
Landscape will ease me somewhat toward the end.

—Trumbull Stickney

## In the Woods

It's summer overhead,
In all the hills and trees,
But autumn underfoot.
I'm walking through dead leaves,

Deep as a shag rug
On every forest floor—
Leaves from last year's fall
And the fall before.

Green leaves and brown leaves
Move in wind's faint breath.
Over me is life.
Under me is death.

Through the leaves I walk.
Through the maze I strive . . .
Just kicking death around
While I am lost in life.

## On the Plains

One freezing day in January
A hooded woman on the lifeless prairie
Walking, solitary.

Her proud, gaunt face
Seemed in this stark place
Like the lone remnant of some ancient race.

Two unleashed dogs were with her,
Brown as prairie grass in winter.
She stood, a statuary figure,

On a high swell against the louring sky....
Then she was gone, and only I
Remained, crestfallen, with continuing eye.

## Two Trees

Left in the cold outdoors, misshapen, stunted,
It is the Christmas tree that no one wanted.
Nature looks to have taken pity on it;
The snow she sent, at first as dull as dust,
Now sparkles like tinsel off its frozen crust.
She's even hung some homemade ornaments:
A crinkled oak leaf, barely hanging on,
Has just unhooked itself and drifted down
To settle where the fir-tree snags have caught it,
And there are other limbs where leaves have blown.
And look! A bright-red cardinal flies far
From its warm nest, and perches on the crest
To play the role of angel or of star.

The tree's owner, a fragile white-haired lady,
Stands and studies the crooked evergreen,
Her window like a mirror in between....

# Decoy

Whenever I see it, pink and fake,
Floating on a pond or lake,
I feel a little envy-ache.

It drifts without a rudder.
It bears no memory of a martyred mother.
And evil couldn't make it shudder.

Nor does it lose a single quill
Attracting birds that hunters kill,
With sly eye and smirking bill....

O to be that swan, with never
A sore foot or a ruffled feather,
And head unbowed no matter what the weather!

# Sunday-Morning Quarterback

When I was a teenager,
My church
Was *CBS News Sunday Morning*,
And its sun-face was my God.
Even in the 80s
The show seemed obsessed with Vietnam.
I remember the stock footage
Of reporters dressed like fighters, running for cover;
Our troops, stealthy, wading across a river;
A cold male narrator
Reading a soldier's sweetheart's last love letter;
Blood-smeared doctors;
Stretchers loaded onto helicopters;
Unpeaceful protesters;
And poorly cut clips in washed-out color
Of the President—the fat-faced Godfather—
Embattled but safe at home, defending the whole endeavor....
All, all of whom should have known better.

They say a child shall lead them: How can we
If we are not consulted?
I sat there angry as a general
Who is usurped and told later
His people have done the wrong thing....

# Tightrope

A high rope-bridge from ridge to ridge,
A cloud bank, and below,
A deep ravine of evergreen.
I walked, unsure and slow.

The rising breeze increased unease.
I clung to rails of rope,
Moving slowest where it was lowest,
And holding on to hope.

After much grasping, slipping, gasping,
I reached the other side.
A lightning crack! *You must go back!*
And with this thought, I died.

## Anastasia's Boy

"Child, come back—" his mother calls, cajolingly,
Standing in the doorway, with the same tone
She uses when she calls him in for supper,
Inviting him to death. "Don't worry, ma'am,
We won't hurt him," says the man in uniform.
It will be painless, as his father's was,
As hers will be. Her husband is still slumped
Over his desk the way she often found him
At dawn after he'd sweated through the night,
Writing his polemic against the state.
The army man sprays something in her hair.
"What does that do?" she wonders, knowingly.
"You'll see." But she can not see anything:
She is already dead…. And now the child
Is running even faster for his life
Down the steep valley of his parents' farm,
His heart exploding. Is this what's meant, he asks,
By the Valley of the Shadow of Death?
He remembers the movie he saw once
About the Russian girl whose folks were killed.
*Anastasia*…. She lived! She lived, didn't she?

## Lighthouse Murder

It offered light that was as boldly bright
As evening star or satellite.
But now it's ancient, dusky, hollow-eyed,
A piece of local history
Preserved by some society.

To one who'd grown up in its scope,
Who'd given up on life and hope,
It seemed as purposeless as he.
They'd lost their lights concurrently....

It was a cold, bleak sea.
He stood beneath his eyeless friend
And heard her voice upon the keening wind:
"I might have saved a ship or two
From wrecking on a bar or bank,
But I could not save you....
I lit the night, the world. Now look at me:
I can't do anything but be."

"Goodbye," he said, then sank
And lay down in the darkness of the sea.

## Dark Place

I look down at the forest floor.
Here there are more
Branches and leaves
Than on the trees,
And in the water running by
There is more white than in the sky,
And more blue in one forget-me-not
Than in a human eye.

I try, I do try
In the outside world to go
From low to high,
Or at least to what is level with my eye.
Here, though....

How perfect this spot would be
For the humble and shy,
Who cannot look their brothers in the eye,
Who seem to find no solace in the sky,
Who share my dark propensity to go
From high to low.

## Private Road

We used to have the mountain to ourselves.
Now every other year some lot is cleared
Above us or below, some house is built
For summer use by bored Floridians.
We hear a little of what is going on
(The sound of saws) and see a little more
Through beeches driving by (cement trucks, backhoes,
A scab that looks more like a house in ruins
Than the solid structure of a future home).

A season later, when the work is done,
We'll go on foot to peer through drapeless windows,
Or stand on empty porches, taking in
The curious view, so different from our own.
(We flee like burglars if we hear a car.)
Lingering in the firefly-dotted dark,
We're held by the pungent smell of new-house wood,
The breeze, the heavens crowning us with stars.
Our dog says when.... Silent, we walk home eased.
The house is ours. The mountain is ours again.

# The Old Logging Road

Oaks and birches block the path
That cuts this little wood in half.
And since there are no loggers anymore
These felled trees will always stand their ground.
But it's no trouble to go around.

Of course, there is the main road far more traveled,
Well-maintained and graveled,
Where I can stroll with happiness and ease,
And not be stopped by trunks of trees.

But since the forest is missing men,
And the path is becoming wood again,
I'll walk this perfect space
For those who like to deviate a little,
But need some kind of anchor down the middle.

# Mountain Development

How long will it be
Before the path is gone,
Cleared, graded,
And gravel piled on?

A hundred years ago
Men carried loads
Of logs to build houses
Over these roads.

A hundred years later
The same kinds of men
Have come to turn the trails
Into roads again.

Soon signs will forbid
And a gate will block
The pleasure of
Our evening walk.

White-ringed blacksnakes
Will stretch across
A bed of gravel
Instead of moss.

Wrens will dig deeply
For worms in ruts,
As squirrels, puzzled,
Comb rocks for nuts.

But streams will still laugh
Whenever they fall,
And wind will make
The same sad call....

How long before they come,
Re-sew the seam,
And build here, just to live
Our summer dream?

## The Stand-in

Why did he always leave his hoe
Standing tall in the furrowed field,
Tall as himself, but planted so,
Not even a storm could make it yield?

He could've easily let it drop
To mark the spot where he'd left off
Hoeing, before he had to stop
To tend the fences or brim the trough.

Behind the food at market and stand
Were still the farmer and his hoe,
Were aching back, and sweat, and blistered hand.
Perhaps he wanted the world to know.

## After Rain

I judge as harshly as the pelting rain.
I don't let up. And if I had my way,
I'd batter all the flowers I never liked,
So badly they would never rise again.

But even floods subside. The sun comes out,
And Nature kisses what it tried to kill.
I weaken. Roses pelt me with their scent
And colors even brighter than before.

## High-flying Boy

Flowers are dancing on their graves.
The hollows feel like drafty caves.
I'm surfing on the wind's big waves.

Usually I stand and gawk
At a bevy or a flock.
But now I'm soaring like a hawk!

And like the hawk I cry aloud,
Evil-eyed and overproud,
As I career from cloud to cloud.

What makes my spirit spring elate
Is my belief that I am great,
That only sheep are slaves of Fate.

I look with pity on the Earth,
Where men are catalogued from birth,
Where some must kill to prove their worth....

I've flown through Poles and back around!
I see the lights of my hometown.
My mother calling brings me down.

## Primitive Mourners

"Why, he fairly grieved himself into the grave! ...
Sad, when mothers are all that some men have....
All hollow-eyed, and skinny as a feather! ..."
This was the talk before the pastor prayed.
He used to come in any kind of weather,
With flowers. I'd watch him kneel and rise and stand,
Thinking of when Neanderthals began
To bury their dead with ceremony, grace,
And human tears rolled down the savage face:
Tenderly they placed the clubs and bones that slayed
Beside their owners in chambers crudely made,
Sealed them, and then departed.... But one stayed,
A son perhaps, whose cries of animal pain
Echoed for days, through the cold, the dark, the rain.

## Islands

Always those island stories,
Islands with buried treasure—
The books that boys with dollar signs for eyes
Would read with keenest pleasure.

And dreams of finding island gold themselves
Also gave them pleasure.
But some boys hid a different dream. To them
The island was the treasure.

## Private Meeting

Five deer were gathered for a private meeting
This evening at the bottom of the lawn.
I opened the back door and yelled a greeting:
The buck let out a snort, and all were gone.

A hunter, then, for trophy or for table,
Might have unleashed his rifle's dormant power.
A nodding grandmother, if she were able,
Might have stayed up to watch them for an hour.

An artist might have taken brush or pencil
And drawn them in the beauty of the season.
But I'm the fiend, the aberrant, the rebel.
I violated Nature for no reason.

## Snow Walk

It gives us now a little guiding-light,
Like a thick midnight forest's silver birches,
Or sculptured saints in empty darkened churches,
Or a black cavern's sparkling stalactite.
It gives each path an unextinguishable light,
Like even unspoiled sand on stormy shores,
Or a dark deserted mansion's marble floors,
Or a black cavern's gleaming stalagmite.

No rays pierce through tonight from moon or star;
No lamps illuminate our graveled lane;
The glow is out in hearth and window-pane;
And at this hour you'd never see a car.
The only light is from the settled snow.
In this dark world it's all the light we know.

# A Winter Memory

I remember the house that seemed resigned to snow.
The mountains, though, were always self-possessed,
Like Persian cats at rest. And over me
A little hollowed-out and nimbused star
So suffocated in a sky of white
That I could stare it down and keep my sight!

I played and sledded, warming to the cold.
The distant rumblings of a plane were heard,
But not the sounds of any other bird.
Two feet of snow, and school was out for weeks!
And frozen still were all the streams and creeks.
Each day it was the same Narnia view.

My childhood then seemed fixed and frozen, too....

# World of Water

On summer days there is a haze
That softens all the hills;
It blues and blurs the oaks and firs,
And like a sea it fills

To the hills' rims, then overbrims
To make a watery sky,
Where real birds and steel birds
Swim instead of fly....

Clouds in motion like foam on oceans,
Shacks like a sunken town,
Banks of laurel like reefs of coral:
If you go out, you'll drown.

A child again before the pane,
I'm watching, deaf and dumb.
My fingers pass along the glass
Of an aquarium.

## Summer Vacation

The cut grass is left in perfect rows,
Like the lines of poetry and prose
The boy remembers while he mows.

The heat, the snapping of the motor,
The gas's and the grass's odor
Recall "Noon Wine" and Larkin's "The Mower".

He learns in his reprieve from school
A sense of Nature's push-and-pull,
That life is hard but beautiful....

As he tires he pictures sitting
In a porch chair, limeade-sipping,
With breezes blowing and flies flitting,

Admiring his work in the summer lighting
And reading what he's now reciting,
Reading those perfect rows of writing.

## For S.B.

After 10<sup>th</sup> grade you left us suddenly,
The kid that everybody seemed to like.
I missed you in the lunchroom, in P.E.,
And passing you on weekends on your bike.

I'd see your old house from the tennis courts
And think sometimes, hitting against the wall,
*I wonder what he's doing at this moment.*
*I wonder if he thinks of us at all….*

You're 50 now, and just as far away—
My new and ever-active Facebook friend.
I read about your exploits, gauge your smile.
I cannot miss you now, as I did then.

## Blue Ridge

The old folks look at the mountain view:
Black to gray to green to blue.
For them there's nothing else to do....

Haven't you ever thought it strange
Something as fixed as a mountain range
Should be the scene of so much change?

Explorers here, in their furthest view,
Saw six or seven rows of blue.
Today we see just one or two.

And Nature offers no solution.
Not all the hues of her ablution
Could rid this land of Man's pollution.

Forget the diesel and the stack:
The hill's still there. The old sit back
And watch it go from blue to black.

## Red-tailed Hawk

The hawk is flying low tonight,
Which means it's going to be cold tonight,
And so I'm going out tonight
Just to watch him fly.
He gets a bum rap
For his predatory habit
Of seeking out some poor innocent rabbit
Then swooping down to grab it
With his snaky talons.
He's just a programmed agent on a mission
For our ecosystem,
Keeping things in balance.
And since all's in jeopardy
From fossil fuels and rising seas,
I'm going out tonight to gawk
At him, to hear him squawk,
To say my nightly prayer for the hawk,
The rabbit, and the water, and the trees.

# The Facing Hills

The hills have faces just like ours—
White from fear, or blushing red,
Shadowy with a secret,
Till noon a sleepyhead!

The hills have sadnesses like mine—
Clouds overhanging for years and years,
Colors hidden under a haze,
A heart of stone, a mist of tears.

And like me, too, the hills at night,
Erased beneath the stars....

## Little Ridge

It was beautiful enough
With all its crags and trees,
And clumps of wild azalea,
And the drowsy sound of bees.

But it was not *this* beautiful,
And lovers never came
Till someone gave it character
By giving it a name.

## The Sign

The sign said LITTLE RIDGE,
But it was falling down,
The letters green and faded
Like the trees around,
That brilliant August day,
The day we moved from town.

Green signs are everywhere
Today, for 9-1-1,
On all the roads with houses,
On some with only one!
It's August on the ridge again.
But the sign is gone.

# The Spirit of the Rose

If one should ascertain at last
The secret of the spirit that impels
The root, the stem, the blossom of the rose,
The garden rose, the universal rose....

Meanwhile the spirit of the rose, knowing not
The meaning of itself, nor even
The meaning of a meaning,
Impels the rose regardless of the rose,
And of the rose that knows.

## Truck Care

I'd never thought of it before today.
When side by side with a trucker on the highway,
Instead of coldly passing, as if to say,
"You people are slow and always in my way,"

Instead of speeding down the road of life
So selfishly and single-mindedly,
I did a thing I'd never done before:
I waved at him. And he waved back at me!

## View from the Garden

Rockless, rich with nutrients,
Watered, free from weeds,
This soil is my mother.

I thought it was everyone's mother,
But as spring proceeds
I grow and begin to see
That those beyond the lofty garden fence
Are not like me.

Without a chance,
They struggle and strain and toil.

If they'd only had my soil....

## Silence

We see her in the village, with her shawl
Wrapped close about her and her downcast eyes
That never seem to see or recognize:
We know her son's short story, — we know it all.
We hear it from the elders, those who know
The sad, stooped figure and the reason why
She never says a word or lifts an eye.
We feel it as we watch her come and go.

The hillcrest is a bumpy, rutty road,
Off which, when every afternoon is done,
Will skid and fall the ever-wheeling sun,
A silent wreck of colored blaze and blood.
We know there lies a horror behind the hill:
A scream, a crash, a death, yet all is still.

## A Mother's Comfort

Terrorists flying into towers,
And other threats from foreign powers;
A wasteland where a dark cloud lours,
Where good is stunted and evil flowers....

Twenty years ago he died,
For all the reasons I just described.
The world is a jungle he couldn't have survived.
He's safe from all of it, safe inside.

# Creek Rock

It happened at McLarsen's swimming hole.
They held him under, slowly letting go
Until his body floated on its own,
Riding the rapids to a point unknown.
He hadn't wanted to come in, you know,
Always afraid of rats and moccasins,
Of bruising his shins on hidden rocks and limbs,
Of anyone who might make fun of him.

The boys returned to their activities.
Their favorite one is climbing to a shelf
Close to the rock wall's summit, and then crashing,
With screams, into the rushing creek below.
Why did they drown him, you might want to know?
Because he watched them. Because their shoves and shocks
Had no more power than water over rock.
Because he craved them. Because they could not change him.

## Roadside Example

The news is in the morning wind:
A man with another man has sinned.
"Bring your feathers, and bring your tar.
We know exactly where they are.
And with God's blessing we will purge
From our fair country the counter-urge."

The two men wake to a blinding sun,
Which shines on Man no matter what he's done.
Happiness is in their eyes
Until they hear the approaching cries:
"Preserve, preserve what God has built!"
They flee, but they are caught and killed.

Other feathers are on them now
As the white sun blazes down.
Since no one will give them a grave in the sod,
Let them be kissed by an older god....
An object lesson for all the others!
Men can be haters but never lovers.

# Lockwood

She gave the grave such life:
The moths, the dew-steeped flowers,
The murmuring summer streams . . .
So much like living's idle hours.

Browsing among the headstones,
Lingering in the wind-stirred night,
Lockwood couldn't imagine it
Because it was his life.

Lockwood is one of the principal narrators in Emily Brontë's *Wuthering Heights*.

## Mountain Rain

Just a mountain evening shower,
Like finger-taps above,
But it put out the all-consuming fires
Of summer and the heart's need for love.

Just a mountain evening shower,
The lightest touch of weather,
Has quenched the summer and the rage in me,
And left us pure together.

# Backcountry

All day around the human race,
Incapable of keeping pace,
He dreams of a secluded place—

This spot beside a dark dead creek
No one would stumble on or seek,
Where he goes camping for a week.

He cannot be himself in town.
It's here he lets his hair hang down
Long as the vines and moss around.

Here he savors every minute,
Every note of jay and linnet,
Beside a channel with nothing in it.

For he's its brother, backwoods-bred,
A trickle on a sticky bed,
With no desire to get ahead.

# End of Summer

The locusts in the thickets
And the frogs in the pond
Have nothing on the crickets
Burrowed in the lawn,
Chirping on and on.
Like tinnitus inside my ear
When there's nothing else to hear,
Like the tell-tale heart
Beating loudly in the dark,
They blow their little whistles
Through the dandelions and thistles,
Through the knotweed and the clover,
Over and over....

The ticking second hand on summer's clock,
The madly choiring crickets
Are running out of minutes.

# Kudzu

A serial strangler's on the loose!
But he leaves behind so many clues
And trails and trails of witnesses,
You'd think he could be stopped.

It does no good to call the cops.
But what about the citizens
Who watch his killings from their porches,
Yet never take up scythes or torches
The way they did in times medieval
To root out pestilence and evil?

Never flagging, never sleeping,
He's always creeping, creeping, creeping,
Coolly planning his next transgression,
Quickly taking full possession.

A serial killer's on the loose,
And beauty is his ruse.
It's gained him quite a following
Of sleuths and lookie-loos.
Beauty can get away with murder.
And there's all of life to lose!

## Little Bridge

Why this bridge across the brook,
These two short slabs of knotted wood,
On which we've never walked or stood?

They join the forest with the lawn.
They start the trail we can't walk on,
So overgrown it's almost gone.

The cracked boards I'm sure would break
Under our increasing weight.
Too fat to leap, too scared to wade!

Brave men bitten by snakes and midges
Who forded rivers that had no bridges,
Who climbed these hills and stood on ridges,

I see you peeking behind the trees,
Contemptuous of our life of ease.
I hear your laughter in the breeze.

## Battle Cry

Today I heard the scream of a bird.
It sounded like the cry
Of an Indian chief with a crazed belief
That in battle he could not die.

This is the spot where the Cherokee fought
With arrow and knife and gun.
Their lives were lost. Their lands were lost.
And their spirits have dwindled to one.

And I could hear it! O feathered spirit
Whose war is never done,
Let loose your cry on this field of sky
And charge the whitest sun.

## Great Spirit

Although your omnipresence
Is world-renowned,
Your soul I never sense
On city ground.

Only among country trees
And freshest air,
In the midst of Nature's raucous peace
I feel you there.

# Dead in the Water

The sea is no more sea
Than its azure dome,
Which is no less white
Than the sea with foam.

I'm thinking of Appalachia,
With its hills like swells,
And its breezes like the sound
Heard on shores and shells.

I'm thinking of the Sahara,
An endless wavy land.
Oases in the sand are water,
But on the sea they're sand....

The undertow has swept me
Too far out of reach!
There is no plane or beacon.
There is no boat or beach.

Similes are pretty, soothing,
Like a Chinese fan.
But water is just water
To a drowning man.

## Turkey Day

Thanksgiving night. A little tired
From all the food and talk, I looked outside.
A band of wild turkeys was on the lawn,
Like a wagon train crossing the Great Divide.

They, too, were searching for the Promised Land,
Someplace out of danger:
A spot for them to squat and not be shot,
Some peaceful forest protected by a ranger.

I longed to be excused and follow them,
To brave the perils of the mountain dark,
And hide with them and live with them forever
Within the smoky Eden of the Park....

"What are you thinking of?" my mother asked,
With all eyes at the table fixed upon me.
"Oh, nothing. Just how grateful that I am
For home and family...."

## Mountain Metropolis

The country is a city too, you know.
The wild geese sound a lot like honking horns.
The logging roads and trails are all dark alleys.
The summer homes invite you in like stores.

You scan the leaves like pages in a bookshop
On trees you'd find in any arboretum.
A hunter's shot could be an engine's backfire,
And every yard's a classic-car museum.

Eat blackberries at the meadow's breakfast bar,
Drink water from a fountain, rest on rock
No harder than a park-bench. Then look up:
The time is told you by that shimmering clock.

It's just like having London for a day
All to yourself, or Paris for a night.
Put down your cell: take in its blazing tower!
The stars come on at once like city lights.

## Burning Bush

Human hands can shear me down
To one inch off the ground,
But I recover and rebound.
In autumn, human heads
Are rapt in other reds.
In winter, I look depressed and dead.
Through spring,
I'm just another greening thing.
But then ...
The heat of summer generates some sparks;
The breezes breathe on them.
And I return to burn again.

# Horsepower

I wonder where it is now—
That truck we bought to get us up the road
In winter, with a tarped and heavy load
Of boxed groceries,
After it iced or snowed.
Even with the pedal floored,
It couldn't do more than 30 miles an hour.
Hanging off the warped running board,
I prayed to the Lord
That a chugging, snapping, backfiring 50s Ford
Would make it up the hill.
*I think I can, I think I can….*

I wonder if it's in some junkyard still….

# Backroad

It went unplowed and unmaintained,
Even after snows and rains
Sank it, or brought a maple down
That blocked our only way to town.
It wasn't wide enough to pass.
Its centerline was weeds and grass.
Ungated, it invited tourists,
Hunters, bikers, or just the curious.
And on the trailheads, late at night,
Lovers parked and killed their lights.

O men and women of Northern cities
Cuddling with your vested kitties,
Who think all Appalachian people
Speak in tongues beneath a steeple,
Who picture panthers in these hills
And hollers hiding moonshine stills,
What brings you to these parts
In your fancy rental cars?
Why are you itching now to travel
On Southern dirt and Southern gravel?

## Pleading Flower

Whether it's cool or hot,
A sunny or a shady spot,
Blooming in fields or forest rot,
There they are, and in one voice they say,
"Forget me not!"

Untouched as in the wildwood,
They flutter even without a breeze.
They try their best, but who'd pick these
For a wife's or a lover's bouquet?
Not even a child would
For his mother's bouquet....
Common as grasses,
And yet they say,
"Forget me not."

Do not sneer, O human masses!
They're only saying the thing you say,
Every day,
As silently as they.

## Hooray for …

All those movies from the 50s
Full of light and hope—
Quaint towns with old clock towers,
Pastel dresses, skirts of flowers
On a May pasture slope,
And cherry trees in CinemaScope….

And a TV special from '59,
*America Pauses for Springtime*—
Choirs, flags, and at the end
Jane Wyman reading the loveliest lines
That Dickinson ever penned:
A light exists in spring….

*Bus Stop, East of Eden,*
*Love Is a Many-Splendored Thing*—
The optimism of the 50s
Before the darker 60s….

And I was born in '69!—
Nostalgic for a time that wasn't even mine….

For nothing gave me so much hope
As cherry trees in CinemaScope.

# The Premiere of *The Yearling* (1946)

After all the years of rearing
Of the fawn into a yearling,
After where the plot was veering
And the scene we knew was nearing
Of the death we had been fearing,
Still the shotgun's shot was searing
On the heart as on the hearing,
Still the audience was tearing.

After dreams of boy and yearling
Playing and careering
Through the forest and the clearing,
After lachrymose veneering
And full-symphonic tiering,
At The End, instead of jeering,
All the audience was cheering
For this story so endearing.

# Cinematographers

For tint, tone, texture and technique
They win the ultimate prize in their profession.
But don't the landscapes that they film deserve
At least an honorable mention?

## Boy in Winter

A wind like a car rushed by,
Sweeping the snow like dust.
And I watched through the frosty window
What would again be lost.

A spirit indifferent and free,
Intent on exploring the world,
Whirled through the woods and vanished,
And suddenly I was cold.

The streams were locked in ice.
The dens were sealed in snow.
But my soul was running, running
With the wind where I cannot go.

## Blood Moon

The scarlet moon is rising
Over Thompson's Ridge.
A boy runs home, dials 9-1-1,
And yells, "A fire is on the ridge!"

The operator calms him
As through the screen he sees
The full moon like a loosed balloon,
And feels the evening breeze....

Quenched and comforted by age
And the balmy scents of June,
The fire of youth dies down to sleep
Beneath the scarlet moon.

# The Coming Night

Poets say the night is like
The dark hair of a woman falling,
Her eager heart is like the nightbird calling,
Her scents are all the blooming trellised flowers,
Her bedroom eyes the stars.

And this is how
I see her on this warm and windy night.
She wants to love me now.

# Contemplation

A purple cloud against a pink sky hovers
Over the dark green mountains in the west.
The sun is gone, and night's first shadow covers
Our little bowl, and puts the birds to rest....
The moon and stars come out, and every bough
Is lit with them. The noisy stream unwinds.
When Man stands in the midst of Nature now,
It is a mystic meeting of the minds.

Like him, the universe is thinking,
And wears a face of stone.
But as he stands beneath the vastness
Of its nocturnal dome,
Man can no more read its thoughts
Than he can know his own.

# Nightlights

The only lights this starless night
Are from two houses on the hill,
Brighter now, for the rain has stopped,
And steadier, now that trees are still.

I stare at them. They stare at me.
Side by side, with a friendly glow,
They fascinate me more
Than any eyes I know.

# Freshman

Just off one of the deeper forest tracks
A solitary Catesby's trillium grows,
Hidden in brush and by her own green bracts,
The wallflower of the woodland, blushing rose.
But where is that boy who came here every day
To love her? Has he found another girl?
For hours, even in showers, he would stay,
Stroking each passive petal like a curl....
So shy by daylight, imagine how closed in
Upon herself in moonlight she must be,
Opening now for no one, even him,
Who comes tonight to nestle virginally
Beneath her delicate head with dewdrops pearled.
Next morning he must leave for the cold world.

## College

I went to sleep with certainty
Of far-succeeding days
When light would show again to me
The hills where I was raised.

It was as if some magic hand
Had moved me in the night,
For I awoke in a foreign land
Without a hill in sight.

It was as if they'd used me
To execute a plan,
For overnight, unwillingly,
I had become a man.

## Alter Ego

My family settled here when I was five.
The boxwood then was struggling to survive
On parched and long-abandoned property.
With very little money, so were we.

The bush was just my height, at 3 foot 3.
I felt a kinship with it instantly.
I watered it, and it came back to life....

We grew together. By the time I graduated
From high school it was over six feet tall,
Like me, with aspirations and swelled head.
I left for college, with a sense of dread....

When I came home for Christmas, it was small
As a dwarf shrub, mercilessly sheared.
But I was not surprised.
The unknown world that I had always feared
Had cut me down to size.

## Tableau

A green leaf and a brown leaf, side by side,
On an old oak we walked together past,
The walk I sensed somehow would be our last,
In early autumn, just before you died.
The two leaves seemed the perfect metaphor
That day, for what we were: a grey-haired lady
Who stooped a bit and was approaching 80,
Beside her son (I'd just turned 44).
Your cheeks were flushed as you were laughing, talking,
And pointing out the wonders that you saw—
The mist, the leaves. Your joy made me withdraw.
I drooped and lagged: I was so tired from walking….
I see us now, amid the autumn scene,
Myself the dead brown leaf, and you the green.

# Octogenarian

It's time to clean the reservoir and spring.
She does it twice a year—
Raking, mopping, panting, stopping . . .
And then the water's clear.

She's always careful going down the steps:
They're either slippery rocks
Or splitting slabs of wood
Or crumbling cinder blocks.

Everyone talks about the uphill journey
Or of being lost and circling round and round.
But she knows, as she grasps the wobbly rail,
It's hardest going down.

# The Carriage (1800s)

A small village under a setting sun,
And the sound of a carriage drawing near;
Four yellow flowers on the side of a road,
  And three deer.

Three deer sleeping on a forest bed
Beside a village under a setting sun;
A rickety carriage, running over three flowers,
  And sparing one.

One yellow flower on the side of a road,
And three deer sleeping on a forest bed;
But two are waking from a carriage noise,
  And one is dead.

I would not ask for a deer from the forest.
I would not take him from his forest abode.
But I will pick one lonely flower
  By the road....

A small village under a rising sun,
And two deer waking to a bright spring day;
And the rickety carriage that left me a flower
  Is gone away.

# The Path to the Clearing

It winds like the path we take
Through the maze of the mind. Down both sides
Vanguards of birches like opposing arguments
Wage silent war. The trail is littered with their leaves
And curled pieces of bark like thoughts cast off
By a mind never ceasing to perfect itself.
Go deeper, and the vast sky dwindles
To a pale blue china bowl with a foliage rim.
And then the end:
The philosophical conclusion,
That clearing where the sun
Rains unimpeded, and you stand in a pillar of light ...
The reason they ask,
*If the way is dark, how can he always come back*
*With shining eyes?*

## Last Ride

Men paved the way for power lines,
In a manner of speaking, by cutting pines,
Carving a pathway straight and wide,
Like the clearing beneath a chairlift ride.

I always wished there were a ride
Up and down that mountainside,
Not for ruby mines or skiing,
But simply for the joy of seeing,
Without the sweat of tiring hikes
Or the revs of motorbikes.

Like kings of old on outside thrones
Smoothly borne by silent drones,
I, too, will have my kingly ride
After I have died,
Floating, not through Heaven or Space,
But over a familiar place
Just for a day, then, like a kite,
Reeled in and folded up for night.

## At Road's End

When I was little, I liked to stand
At the intersection that we called
"The Four Corners".
The gravel roads diverged from it
Like spokes on a wagon wheel.
One road ran into the woods and stopped.
One climbed over a hill then dropped.
One wound round and round along a ridge.
One went townward, over a bridge.
(There was a fifth road, too, but no one counted it
Because it ended in a quicksand bed.)

A poet chose between two roads.
But if I'm not mistaken,
There are many choices and roads not taken,
And all of them end in a quicksand bed.
And on the one we take, for most of us,
There's not a trace of tread.

(By the way, beside that quicksand bed,
A trillium grew—a real natural wonder.
I plan to keep my eyes on it
When I am going under.)

## Grave-House

"Your father's been to Grave-House," I heard my mother say.

"Are we to settle there?" I asked, in a curious way.

"Oh, someday.
It is a beautiful place, with flowers all around;
A stone with an inscription, at the entrance, on the ground;
And many other houses scattered round."

I pictured the place in my mind....

That was many winters ago.
We traveled there in silence
Through a storm of snow.

Now, I know.

## Thank-Yous

Thank you to poets Danita Dodson and Shelby Stephenson for their "blurbery," as Fred Chappell called it. Dr. Chappell, who endorsed my two previous books, passed away in January, 2024. I valued his criticism even more than his praise. Throughout my short publication history I have discovered that Southern poets, like Southern people, are the most hospitable in the world.

Thank you to publishers Kevin Walzer and Lori Jareo for taking me on a third time.

And thank you to my mother, who emailed these words to me many years ago: "You have a strange and unique mind…. And your eyes always look like they're on the verge of some great discovery."

## About the Author

Allen Ireland moved from the Rockies to the Smokies in 2023 and is happy to be back among the landscapes of his youth. He welcomes feedback from readers and can be contacted at allenleeireland@outlook.com.

Made in the USA
Columbia, SC
25 July 2024

38719987R00052